THE CHANGING [

Bicester

BOOK ONE

Peter Barrington

Robert Boyd
PUBLICATIONS

Published by
Robert Boyd Publications
260 Colwell Drive
Witney, Oxfordshire OX8 7LW

First published 1998

Copyright © Peter Barrington and
Robert Boyd Publications

ISBN: 1 899536 30 2

OTHER TITLES IN THE *CHANGING FACES* SERIES

Printed and bound in Great Britain at The Alden Press, Oxford

Contents

Front cover photograph

Arthur Butler's Covent Garden Fruit Stores.

Back cover photograph

A celebration of Queen Victoria's diamond jubilee, 1897.

Acknowledgements

Many people responded to my appeal through the Bicester Advertiser for old photographs and information for this book.

I am grateful to them and other people I contacted in the town.

Such was the wealth of material offered that a second volume is planned and some photographs have been held over for Book Two.

If anyone has material they would like to submit for the second volume I can be contacted c/o Bicester Advertiser, 50 Market Square, Bicester, Oxon, OX6 7AJ.

I would like to thank the following for their help and loan of material — and I apologise if anyone has been inadvertently left out: Lt Col John Connelly, David Watts, John Watts, Michael Morgan, Harry Hovard, Arthur Hollis, Frank Wood, David Waller, Wilf Smith, Michael Waine, the Rev Philip Ball, Evelyn Clayton, Emma Friman, Michael Nicholson, Gordon Allen, Henry Evans, Andrew Banks, Brian Penhallow, William and Grace Cherry, Mrs A Painter, Tom Martin, Doris Martin, Esme Timms, Roger Thomas, Tony Bowne, Rod Bourton, William Nash, Trevor and Graham Nash, Sue Quainton (of Bicester Community College), Joe Launchbury, Connie Harris, Eileen Clark, Maurice Alley, Anthony Hedges, Fiona Stuart and Mrs P. Barney.

I am also grateful to the Bicester Advertiser.

Preface

There have been two earlier books of photographs depicting Bicester in years gone by — Bicester in Camera (published in 1986) and Bicester and Otmoor in Old Photographs (1992).

And there was the celebrated *Bicester Wuz a little Town* by Sid Hedges, which has been reprinted twice since its original publication in 1968.

For those wanting a more scholarly history of Bicester there is Dunkin's History of Bicester and the Victoria County History of Oxfordshire.

In compiling this volume *The Changing Faces of Bicester* — one of a series covering various communities in the county — I have endeavoured to cover in greater detail aspects of town life that were touched upon in the two earlier photograph based books.

However, some duplication is unavoidable, though photographs common to the other two books have been used sparingly.

Where the other volumes showed, for example, the Hedges block of shops, I have been able, with help from families, to record the people who lived and worked on the premises.

I have also gone outside the Bicester parish to include a section on Bicester Ordnance Depot, which has had a big impact on the town through housing and employment.

For a projected second volume I hope to include RAF Bicester and other aspects of Bicester town life such as the Roman Catholic church, which are not included here.

I have also in this volume looked briefly at agriculture as Bicester was and is a market town.

Peter Barrington
August, 1998

Bicester Today

Walk round Bicester with an eye for history and you will rapidly come to two conclusions about this Oxfordshire market town.

One is that the town basically began from the ancient central core that takes in the vicinity of St Edburg's parish church, Bicester House, Market Square, The Causeway and Sheep Street.

The other is that Bicester as a whole looks very much like a town that has grown to its present proportions since the end of the 1939-45 war.

In many respects this is the story of many towns these days, not just of Bicester.

For Bicester though, these conclusions are particularly pertinent to the town you see today.

The town has Anglo-Saxon and Roman roots and over the centuries grew gradually with agriculture being the prime industry.

And while there was some housing development between the 1914-18 and the 1939-45 wars, the town's major developments have happened since 1945.

A glance at the town's population figures in a sense tells the story.

In 1931 the population of Bicester was 3,004, in 1951 it was 4,171, in 1961 the figure had grown to 5,513.

A decade later the population had risen to 12,355 in 1971, while in 1981 it had reached 14,4027.

Ten years on there was a leap to 20,241 in 1981 and by mid-1997 the population was 23,858.

All the post-1945 growth is accounted for by the housing developments.

Broadly these were the build-up of the King's End estate just to the west of Queen's Avenue for council housing and housing for workers employed at Bicester Ordnance Depot.

There was housing development on either side of Churchill Road — a mix of council and private sector housing.

One of the first of the newer housing estates was built on King's End Farm by Greenwood Homes on the western side of town.

At the same time there was a slower build-up of homes on Glory Farm off Churchill Road.

Southwold housing estate was built on the site of South Farm, between Buckingham Road and Banbury Road, from the early 1990s and Langford Village on the southern side of the town from roughly the same period.

The latest estate is on Slade Farm, bounded by Banbury Road, Lord's Lane and the embankment of the London-Bicester-Banbury-Birmingham railway line.

Work began at Slade Farm in late 1997.

The rapid growth of Bicester since 1945 was planned. Until 1979 the direction of growth in Oxfordshire was handled through Oxfordshire development plans and from 1979 through the Oxfordshire structure plan, a system which is followed throughout the country.

It was through these long-term plans — that have to be agreed by the relevant government department, most recently the Department of the Environment — that Bicester has been shaped.

The strategic policy of these long-term plans was to direct most of Oxfordshire's housing growth to the county or market towns — Bicester, Banbury, Witney, Abingdon, Didcot and Wantage/Grove — to take the pressure off the city of Oxford. The city itself accepted growth with the Blackbird Leys estate and much housing on what are called urban renewal sites.

Coupled with Bicester's housing expansion has been a growth in industry.

The former Bicester Urban District Council obtained government permission for the sites beside Launton Road to be developed for industry, to give more job opportunities to people in the town and district, who had previously relied on the car factory complex at Cowley, Oxford, and the Ordnance Depot in Bicester.

One of the earliest arrivals was Bruce Engineering (now LEAK) and other companies came in anticipation of the completion of the M40 motorway between Waterstock, outside Oxford, to Warwick and the Birmingham motorway network. The M40 extension through Oxfordshire was opened in January, 1991.

Bicester's retail area has expanded too.

The largest development in recent years was the building through private enterprise of the Crown Walk shopping mall, which opened in 1988. It was built on mainly semi-derelict land between Market Square and Sheep Street.

Bicester Village retail discount shopping centre opened in 1995.

The story of Bicester is also bound up with the military.

Alchester, the Roman town, was really a garrison fort built on low land between Wendlebury and the present day Bicester and served by the Roman Road of Akeman Street, which runs from Cirencester to St Albans, and another Roman Road running from Dorchester on Thames towards Towcester.

There were two major airfields. Both RAF Upper Heyford and RAF Bicester date from the 1914-18 war and during the 1939-45 war there were small satellite airfields at Finmere and Shelswell Park.

Bicester Ordnance Depot was built from 1941 when the government was preparing for the re-invasion of Europe on what became known as D Day, June 6, 1944.

These advertisements have been reproduced from the souvenir booklet published to mark the Bicester and District Chamber of Commerce Empire Shopping and Carnival Week, 20th-25th July, 1931. They serve as an introduction to the sections in this book on Sheep Street and Market Square.

SECTION ONE

Sheep Street

Sheep Street has been for centuries one of Bicester's main thorougfares.

For many years a weekly livestock market was held in the street. But in 1906 the former Bicester Urban District Council was pressed by the Board of Agriculture to improve the surface.

The UDC — which ceased in the 1974 re-organisation of local government — decided to build a cattle market on land off Victoria Road. The market was opened on a site of just under two acres in 1910.

Sheep Street became part of the A41 trunk road from London to Birkenhead and became busier with the growth of traffic.

The increasing flow of traffic and size of lorries led to the demolition of the Hedge's block that stood in the middle of Market Hill and the road in 1963. This gave traffic a clear run in either direction.

After the Bicester by-pass — Boundary Way — was built between London Road and Oxford Road a day-time traffic ban was introduced in Sheep Street in 1992.

This was followed by a full pedestrianisation by Cherwell District Council in 1994 for the section of Sheep Street from the Bell Lane junction to Market Square.

This aerial photograph of Bicester town centre dating from the 1920s or 1930s clearly shows how Sheep Street dominates the scene, running diagonally through the middle.

Market Square — a triangle — can be seen in the centre middle with the Hedge's block on the line of Sheep Street and London Road.

On the left is Victoria Road and on the right of Sheep Street are the gardens that ran down to the Bure brook. On the far right is some of the Bicester House land that became the site of Hanover Gardens old people's flats in 1982. Manorsfield Road, linking Market Square and St John's Street, was built through the site in 1975.

In the top righthand corner is land behind Market Square with Priory Road running left to right.

The market can be seen in full swing in Sheep Street in this postcard that was mailed in 1905.

An unusual photograph of Sheep Street (below) was taken from the central block of buildings in Market Square that overlooks the present day car park. In the centre is the dome of the Midland Bank with the old county court office (now occupied by Alfred Truman, solicitors, on the left). On the other side of the street can be seen Ashmore's ironmongery, which was burnt down in 1969 and re-built. Next door is Lloyds Bank, which is the only building in the street to retain iron railings in the front.

A large private house became a cafe and fruit shop and was eventually de-molished in the 1960s to become the site of Woolworth's.

The tall three-storey building with blind out was Sandiland's chemists shop, founded by Robert Burgess Sandiland in 1832. The business was taken over by J T Mountain in 1902 and run by him and his daughter Dorothy. She carried on her father's business after his death. Dorothy retired in the 1960s but caried on with her work for the Red Cross in Bicester. She completed 73 years with the Red Cross in 1986. She died in 1993 in her 90s. After Miss Mountain retired, the building was demolished and became a supermarket. It is now occupied by Dorothy Perkins and a card shop.

A Temperance Hotel stood next door and adjacent was London House that was once the Bear pub. The shop with a fine facade and a row of three first floor windows was Tom Druce's drapery shop that from around 1900 incorporated London House. Druce's, later Preece, is now Sambrook's.

Another view of Sheep Street dating from the 1950s shows Druce's store that by then was Preece. Next was Waine's butcher's shop.

The Crown Hotel on the left was a social centre as at the back it had the town's only cinema for many years and also the Corn Exchange. The hotel was demolished in 1963 to be the site of the first Tesco store. This in turn made way for the Crown Walk shopping mall that opened in 1988.

An older view of Sheep Street shows elephants and camels heading a circus parade evidently to the delight of children and shoppers.

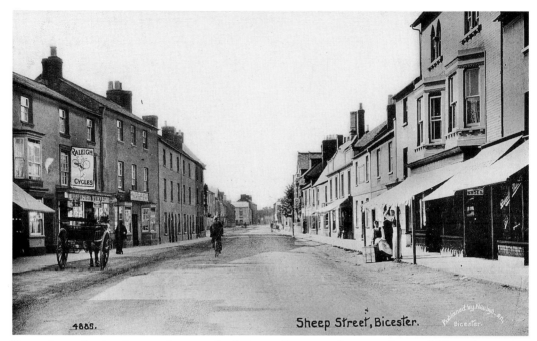

Two views depict the northern end of Sheep Street and were taken within a few years of one another. The first is from a postcard dated 1910. On the right is Norman Prentice's shoe shop with Walt Smith's grocery shop next door.

The second view dates from after 1914 as the Post Office had been built. The Post Office is the large three-storey brick building in the middle of the row on the right. It has a mock Georgian frontage and had a sorting office at the back with an entrance to a van yard of Victoria Road. The sorting office was re-located to Murdock Road in 1992 and the PO closed in 1994 with the PO counters going into Forbuoys shop next door.

The PO building is now the Penny Black pub/restaurant.

Alf Evans's department store was a major retailer in Sheep Street for most of the 20th century.

He founded the business in September, 1902 with this shop (7) on either side of what is now Evans Yard, a small shopping precinct. Alf can be seen in this photograph dated 1906 standing in the centre in front of a pillar. His wife Nellie is believed to be the woman on the left. The shop assistant on the right is believed to be Cyril Walker. The horse and cart was used for deliveries, the horse being stabled in a barn at the back.

Alf moved the business across Sheep Street towards the end of 1917 or at the beginning of 1918. The present occupants of the first site are a clothes shop on the left and Bicester Bakery and Boots on the right of the yard. The precinct was established in 1983.

The new shop was created in 34 and 36 Sheep Street (which was a toy shop run by two spinsters named Smith) and soon after No 38 was incorporated.

This photos and the one on the following page show the new shop in the 1950s/1960s. Although the fronts are similar the first shows the walk-round arcade and the second show the altered frontage put in before 1965. The second picture shows the store decorated for the Queen's visit to Bicester Ordnance Depot and RAF Bicester in 1965.

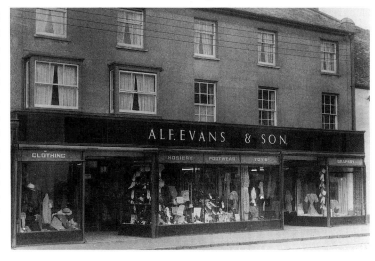

Alf is seen at the back of the original store in the garden that was one of several that ran down to the Bure brook.

Alf and his wife Nellie (back seat, right) are pictured in their car with their family in Evans Yard.

After Alf died in 1956 his son John, who had been in the business all his life, took over running the store. John takes delivery of a lemon yellow Vauxhall Velox car outside the store from Layton's Garage in January, 1961. The car was believed to be one of the first in Bicester that was not painted black.

When John died in 1971 his son Henry became the third generation to run the store. Henry is pictured in the shop with assistants John Blencowe (left) and Stan Naylor in 1978.

 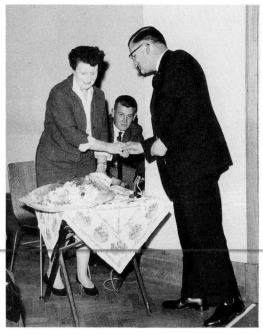

Evan's store went in for promotions and these three photographs are from a fashion show in the Methodist Hall in 1956. Mrs Eileen Clark is modelling on the catwalk and is being thanked by John (Jack) Evans with Michael Lambourne in the background. Five staff model coats on the steps of John Evan's house in Victoria Road (now a veterinary surgery). From the left: Valerie Jones, Jan Blowfield, Margaret Allen, Eileen Clark and Ethel Blowfield, mother of Jan.

The department store closed in 1981 when Henry Evans opened a menswear shop in Market Hill in premises now occupied by Connell, estate agents. Hiltons shoe shop, then located in the Market Hill building, moved into Evans's former premises.

The Handy Stores were founded in Sheep Street in 1923 by William Cherry and his wife Grace. They sold hardware, including pot menders and boot studs.

The street at the time was a mixture of houses, cottages, inns and shops. The weekly market was held in the southern end of the street. Opposite the shop and home for the Cherry's was an entrance to a forge with a row of thatched cottages on one side of the forge entrance.

On the other side of the entrance was the residence of Dr Long and every morning a maid would come out to polish the brass knocker and door knob of the front door.

The Handy Stores was located on the left of this photo dated 1897. Diamond Villa, the tall imposing building on the left, was built in 1897. The Handy Stores occupy this house and also the one next door. The house on the extreme left has been demolished and is part of the site of the Methodist Church. On the right is Dr Long's house, the frontage has been retained and incorporated into Tesco's supermarket.

Trinders Motorcycle Shop

Eric Trinder's bicycle and motorcycle shop was a feature of Sheep Street from 1928 to 1981.

Eric is pictured in 1974 (next page) on a moped. He was the fifth of six sons. His father started a Banbury cycle business in 1880 and in the 1920s the four elder brothers set up branches in Bicester, Daventry and Towcester. Eric came to Bicester in 1928 to take over a business in Sheep Street whose proprietor had fallen on hard times. In 1964 he became the first Honda agent in the country.

The business was taken over by the Allington family in 1981, who now call it Broadribbs.

Eric died in 1990, aged 82. He is pictured with his bicycle mechanic of over 30 years Arthur Powell checking over a Penny Farthing, which was one of seven he found in a loft of a cycle shop in Banbury. The Penny Farthing and a collection of other old bikes were given to a cycle museum before Eric retired.

Waine's Butcher's Shop

Waine's butcher's shop at 26 Sheep Street is shown with a fine display of meat on opening day, April 2, 1934.

The property consisted of a large private house with stables, accommodating at least six horses, yard and malthouse and was bought by Harry Havelock Waine from the executors of T Druce and Co — the owners of numbers 22, 25 and 26 Sheep Street — in 1933.

The conversion from a private house to a shop was carried out in six months by a London firm and included the provision of a tiled shop and shopfront and the building of an especially large meat fridge at the back. The meat fridge was thought to be the first in any food shop in Bicester and was essential in keeping meat fresh in the summer months.

The business was run by Harry Waine and his two sons, Fred and Jim, and operated from April 2, 1934, to closing day on October 23, 1969.

Waine's was one of the last family butchers in Bicester. Cattle, pigs and sheep bought weekly at Bicester market and from various farmers in the Bicester area were kept on the premises until killed in the slaughterhouse at the bottom of the yard.

Customers came from as far away as Oxford to buy Harry Waine's brawn and special recipe pork and beef sausages, which he made in the sausage house, which was situated in the yard behind the shop.

During the Second World War with both Fred and Jim away, a meat delivery service was operated by Ernie Jones, Molly Waine, Nellie Byng and Mary Ward took meat by van to the surrounding villages of Ambrosden, Great and Little Chesterton, Marsh Gibbon, Merton, Poundon, Stratton Audley, Twyford and Wendlebury.

The immediate post-war years found meat rationing still in force and the Waine family supplemented their customers' rations by catching wild rabbits on their land at Ambrosden and land of neighbouring farming friends.

Harry Waine (right) is pictured with his son Fred ferreting for rabbits on their land at Ambrosden in about 1948.

For this purpose a narrow leather collar was put around the ferret's neck and a strong line attached to the collar.

The holes to the warren would be blocked with sacks and the ferret would be placed into the burrow. The ferret would hunt and drive all the rabbits usually into one part of the burrow where the ferret would "hold" them. The ferret would be traced through the line to the collar.

Another method was for nets to be pegged outside all the warren exits and the ferret put in without a collar and line. The ferret would drive the rabbits into a net. But sometimes rabbits were lost if they ran fast enough and carried the nets with them as they escaped over a field.

Fifty years or more ago many Bicasterians and village folk kept their own ferrets and local gamekeepers loaned ferrets to the Waine family to give their hunters a work out during winter months.

An old Bicester character, rag and bone man Joe Palmer, of Priory Road, had rabbit skins delivered to his premises by Molly Waine. This saved Joe the trouble of harnessing his horse and cart and collecting the skins with his assistant and nephew Tommy Hill from the butcher's at the Ashton Club yard off Sheep Street and Victoria Road.

The White Hart

Another character of Sheep Street and the town was pub landlady Zena Hinchley of the White Hart.

Zena would welcome newcomers with a loud "Hallo, my darling",

She said of herself that she had "an unusual name for an unusual person." Born in Jericho, Oxford, and was named after the famous actress Zena Dare and was destined to be a barmaid "from the moment I could walk to a barrel in my grandmother's pub".

Her grandmother kept the Fountain Inn at Oxford. During the Second World War Zena became an entertainer in pubs and concert halls in Oxford, singing and playing the piano.

When working in a pub in St Ives, Cornwall, she met and married Alan Hinchley and they moved to the Jericho House pub, Oxford, and then came to the Six Bells, Bicester. After nine years they took over the White Hart, retiring in 1990 after 22 years.

Zena supported many charities at the White Hart, including Bicester Round Table's sponsored wheelride and St Edburg House old people's home ind Old Place Yard.

Alan (left) and Zena are seen with Edith Barber outside the pub before a Round Table wheelride. The pub's team was typically named the White Hart Virgins – Maid to Stay.

Alan died in 1993, aged 62, and Zena died four months later aged 81. In her will Zena left two generous legacies to St Edburg's parish church and Bicester Community Hospital.

Nash's Bakery was founded in 1930 when William Nash came to Bicester after a bakery partnership in St Aldates, Oxford, broke up after three years.

His first shop was in a group of buildings that has since been demolished where the Halifax Building Society stands. The family lived above the shop and the bakery was in the yard behind. Nash's also had a shop in North Street.

About 30 years ago the shop was moved to its present location and by then the North Street shop was closed and the bakery was at the bottom of Priory Road. A new bakery was opened in 1986 nearby. The business also owns Bicester Bakery in Sheep Street and has shops in Oxford covered market, Blackbird Leys in Oxford and Chipping Norton.

William and Winifred had a large family including the seven sons pictured with their parents in April, 1964. At various times all the boys worked in the bakery and were members of Bicester Rugby Club. Here they formed one of the club's two seven a side teams for a tournament at Banbury. They had a bye in the first round and lost in the second.

Standing, from the left: Trevor, Lawrence, Winifred, William, Paul, Stafford; in front: Clive, Cliff and Graham. Trevor and Graham now run the bakery, Lawrence and Cliff ran their Ambrosden shop for a while and later Lawrence opened a jewellers shop in Sheep Street. Clive ran Helene Gail, hairdressers in Sheep Street, for many years. Trevor, Graham, Lawrence and Cliff owned Crystal china and glass shop in Sheep Street for several years. Trevor and Graham now run Nash's Bakery.

Graham and William are pictured at Blackpool in 1998 after Graham became president of the National Association of Master Bakers.

Market Square

Market Square is the hub of Bicester and is the focal gathering pont for many events from the Boxing Day meet by the Bicester Hunt to proclamations, parades and a Royal visit.

The square is triangular and in addition to the present day car park it also incorporates the area on the other side of the central block of shops and offices that is known as Market Hill (dominated these days by a supermarket).

The Market Square, Bicester.   4886.   Published by Newby & Son, Bicester.

Pankhurst's stationery shop is on the left of this view from a postcard dated 1913. Thomas William Pankhurst came to Bicester from Finchley, London, in about 1870 to join the printers E Smith and Co. Mr Pankhurst was responsible for re-launching the Bicester Advertiser in 1879. The newspaper was first published in 1855 but ceased after a while. In 1886 the company was Smith and Pankhurst. The other town newspaper the Bicester Herald was absorbed into the Advertiser in 1917 when the Herald ceased publication. In the early 1970s the title Bicester Advertiser was sold to the present owners based in Oxford.

Next to Pankhurst in the picture is the Cross Keys pub, now occupied by an estate agent.

A view of the Market Square shows the Causeway leading to St Edburg's parish church. The white painted shop on the left is A V Bowne's hairdressers and tobacconists, and on the right is another view of Pankhurst's with a Bicester Advertiser sign on top. Two doors down from Pankhurst's is the Rose and Crown pub and Bridge House. Both were demolished in the late 1960s. The site is now occupied by the National Westminster Bank and other businesses and is also one end of Manorsfield Road.

A London Brick Company flatbed lorry is parked on the Market Square. London Brick had a brickworks at Calvert until it was closed in 1991. On the left next to Bowne's is Wadley's radio shop that moved from The Causeway in 1935.

Market Square in snow depicts the central block. A caption on the back of this postcard view reads: The Wheelbarrow Brigade. Cheap Coal for the poor.

This photograph is dated 1909. Originally the hunt was Bicester and Warden Hill Hunt and became Bicester Hunt with the Whaddon Chase in 1985 following an amalgamation. Warden Hill is north of Banbury.

A large crowd gathers in the square in May, 1910, for the proclamation of the acession to the throne of George V.

Queen Victoria's diamond jubilee in 1897 was celebrated by the firing of anvils.

When Queen Elizabeth 11 celebrated her silver anniversary in 1977 anvils were fired again. The firing was undertaken by the Rev Michael Scott-Joynt, leader of Bicester team ministry, with his curate, the Rev Jonathan Meyrick (left) and the Rev John Blyth (right), who was the member of the team responsible for Launton.

The Queen, accompanied by the Duke of Edinburgh, stopped in Market Square to meet officials of Bicester Urban District Council and a large crowd in May, 1965, between official visits to Bicester Ordnance Depot and RAF Bicester.

Councillor Mick O'Brien is pictured escorting the Queen across the square.

The Queen and the Duke signed photographs of themselves and a visitors book. The clerk to the UDC, the late Raymond Bainton, holds the book pages down. The photographs hang in the council chamber at The Garth, now the offices of Bicester Town Council.

Over the years businesses in Market Square have changed. Robert and Bustin's garage is seen in about the late 1920s. Mrs Phyllis Barney says her father is on the right in shirtsleeves.

"I can remember as a very small girl going to Bicester, we lived at Weston-on-the-Green, on the carrier of my mother's bike, which she left in the garage yard while we went shopping."

Robert and Bustin's ran a taxi service and Mrs Barney recalls that once her father had to meet the Prince of Wales (later Duke of Windsor) at Bicester North railway station and take him to the Bicester Hunt meet at Stratton Audley.

"Another tale he told was how some lady wanted a taxi home. As it was late and he was due to leave work he was rather annoyed, so he drove rather fast and gave her a bumpy ride. Alas, when he opened the door at her destination, the car was empty. In his haste he had driven off without his passenger." said Mrs Barney.

Mrs Barney said her parents were "chapel" and were friendly with many chapel people in Bicester.

"I particularly remember Miss Scrivener, who had a shop two doors away from the garage. Her shop was packed to the ceiling with goods — here my mother bought her wool and she had many toys," said Mrs Barney.

Scriveners shop can be seen in other Market Square photos on the left next to Wadley's.

The garage later became Lambourne's radio and television shop, now occupied by Granada. On the left of the garage was the Red Lion, now Ye Olde Pioneer, and on the right was Lewis's chemists shop.

A celebrated taxi and coach proprietor with a Market Square connection was Albert Taylor, seen at the driver's window of one of his coaches. Albert is pictured in Army uniform. He was in the Royal Electrical and Mechanical Engineers (REME), in the 1939-45 war.

Albert is pictured in coat and cap with two of his coaches.

His claim to fame was winning £147,000 on Littlewoods football pools. In 1960 at the suggestion of councillor Joe Leach he gave a chain of office to the town for the chairman of Bicester Urban District Council.

The chain subsequently became the chain of office of Bicester Town Mayor on creation of Bicester Town Council in the local government amalgamations of 1974. Councillor Mrs Mary May holds up the chain (see next page) at the time in 1992 when town councillors agreed to buy more "lozenges" to extend the chain and for the inscription of more town mayors' names.

Albert Taylor was called Rich Albert after his pools win. He was the son of Dick and Sarah Jane Taylor, who ran the Angel pub in Sheep Street. Dick also had a taxi business at the pub.

When Dick died the pub licence was transferred to his wife. Albert and his then wife Phyllis helped. Albert's sisters, who became Mrs Kathleen Kiernan and Mrs Marjorie Pugh, also assisted.

Albert's wife Phyllis took over the taxi business when they divorced. She ran the business from 50 Market Square, now occupied by the Bicester Advertiser.

Albert ran his coach business from a house and yard in Banbury Road. The house was demolished to open up land that became Taylor Close. Albert also ran what has become The Chase filling station on London Road. He was reputed to have won the pools from an office at 13 Sheep Street (now part of Crown Walk shopping mall).

Wadley's have been on Market Square since 1935. Harry Wadley in 1978, was a pioneer of radio manufacturing and sold the first radios in Oxfordshire. Harry began displaying radios in the window of his father's greengrocery in The Causeway. Harry was a radio operator in the Royal Navy in the 1914-18 war and began making radios in 1919. He bought wooden cases in London for 3s 6d and engraved them The Wadleyphone. He was a founder shareholder in the BBC 1923.

In 1935 he bought the Market Square premises and ceased making radios when mass production took over. Harry died in 1979 aged 80. By then his son John and grandsons were running the business that continues today.

Next door for many years was Alf Bowne's hairdressing salon, tobacconists and perfumery. Alf came to Bicester from Wolverton (now part of Milton Keynes) in 1921, and

is seen outside his Sheep Street shop where later Albert Taylor filled in his prize-winning pools coupon (now H Samuel, jewellers). Alf took over a Market Square hairdressers in 1923 owned by J Hone. In 1930 he closed the Sheep Street shop.

Alf's wife is seen holding their daughter Dorothy (Dot) with an assistant outside the Market Square shop in 1926. Alf and his wife Mabel are pictured in the 1920s after their marriage in 1923. Alf is in cricket clothes as he played for the Bicester Thursday team for shopkeepers whose businesses were closed on Thursday afternoons.

Dot Bowne liked to ride ponies and is pictured on a Shetland in a yard behind Lissetter's shop in 1929-30. Bowne's shop in 1930. Tony, Alf's son, and his wife Chris in their shop in the late 1970s.

Tony's daughter Sarah and his sister Dorothy (Dot) Knight in the 1980s. Dot preferred to cut men's hair and as a young woman many soldiers tried to date her.

"It was always difficult to make arrangements because my father was strict and could listen into our conversations in the salong over an intercom." said Dot. She married a policeman and retired in 1988. Dot died in 1992. When Alf died in 1966 Tony took over the business. Tony and Chris retired in 1997.

One of the features of Bowne's was Toby, a magnficent ginger cat who often slept in the window displays. Toby arrived in 1982 and died in 1997. He is pictured in 1993.

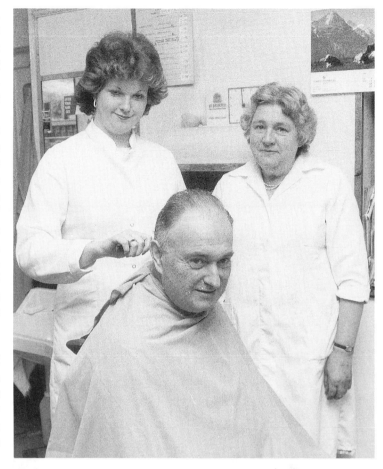

Many people in Bicester followed the career of actor George Rose, who made his name in musicals on Broadway, gaining Tony awards as Doolittle in a revival of My Fair Lady and as the music hall chairman in a musical version of The Mystery of Edwin Drood, from the unfinished novel by Dickens. Another celebrated role was a Major General Stanley in the famed Broadway version of The Pirates of Penzance.

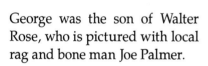

George was the son of Walter Rose, who is pictured with local rag and bone man Joe Palmer.

Walter Rose had a butcher's shop on Market Square in the alleyway next to the present Bicester Advertiser office. George and friends acted out sketches in the attic of the family home with the title: George Rose's Theatre written on the glass of the door.

George was a member of the Red Rhythmics Harmonica Band run from Bicester Methodist Church Sunday School.

When studying music in London George was talent spotted by Laurence Olivier and appeared in character roles at the Shakespeare Memorial Theatre (now Royal Shakespeare Theatre), Stratford.

George appeared in many plays and revues in London and took over the role of the Common Man from Leo McKern in A Man for All Seasons by Robert Bolt. He went to Broadway with Paul Scofield as Thomas More and decided to stay in New York.

He had a long and successful career on Broadway. He bought a villa the Dominican Republic for his retirement. He died in 1988 aged 68 allegedly in a road accident. Despite police investigations his death was never properly explained.

George left money in a trust fund that is able to make grants for maintenance to Bucknell parish church, where there is a commemorative plaque.

Hedges Block

The Hedges Block stood across Market Hill — part of Market Square — with the London to Bicester to Banbury road running round one side, known as The Narrows as it passed the block. The block included Hedges drapery and outfitters, the Covent Garden Fruit Stores and a cafe.

The block was demolished in 1963 to give the growing traffic a straight run. Many townspeople date the change in the town's character from this time.

An unusual photograph shows the other side of the block from the Hedges shop and was probably taken from the roof of Goble's. The end of the central block can be seen and the Midland Bank, which at the time was described on the facade as the London Joint City and Midland Bank. The bank stands on the site of the George inn and the corner is still known as the George Corner.

Two more photographs depict the Hedges shop in greater detail.

John Hedges (1834-1922) was the first member of the family to come to Bicester, circa 1857. He was the son of George and Susan Hedges of Headington, Oxford. John was not in trade to begin with but became a baker in Church Terrace by 1861, and in 1868 he was on Market Square.

John became involved with the Methodist Church and in 1859 was reported to be among those giving a religious address at a public tea on Boxing Day.

John's son was George William Hedges (1862-1936). He married Mary Ann McKay at Bicester Wesleyan Chapel in 1887, and their sons were William John, Sidney George and Cecil Egerton Hedges.

In 1891 there is a reference to a baker's and draper's shop on Market Hill and in 1907 there was the first trade entry in a directory.

Anthony Hedges, son of Sidney George Hedges, writes: "I was very fond of my father's brother Will and his wife, who were very kind to me when I was a teenager, and later to my wife Joy. But there was little love lost between the two brothers, who were as different as chalk from cheese. Will was very relaxed and unassuming; my father was very assertive and ambitious. Their other brother Cecil was killed in a swimming accident whilst (I think) in his late teens. That two; and one had to help with the family business. Will didn't really want to; my father positively refused. That seems to be the crux of the mutual antipathy and although they later lived within a few doors of each other there was little direct contact."

Anthony adds: "If my memory is correct the store was founded by my great grandfather and taken over on his death by my grandfather George. It was an old, large, ramshackle building and even to my young eyes the shop seemed old-fashioned both in style and lack of presentation. The family lived over the shop for a time and were still there when my father returned from the first world war."

Sid and Mary Hedges are pictured in 1959.

Anthony wrote: "My mother's father, George Dixon, was also a shopkeeper. For a long time he managed Hilton's shoe shop, adjacent to the Hedges shop and then he bought The Sweet Shop, an ancient building opposite the Hedges shop. My father's story was that when he was courting my mother he used to play his violin at an open window in the Hedges building and she used to listen from an open window above her father's shop. Innocent times!"

George Dixon and his family are pictured in a typical group ose. The photo is inscribed on the back: Mr and Mrs G H Dixon and family, Dorothy, Mary and Grandma Garbett.

Hilton's shop is seen with the staff, from the left: B Cripps, Annie Grimsley, Euan Wall (relief manager).

Sid Hedges wrote many books often on a theme of activities for young people. But he is most famous as the author of Bicester Wuz a Little Town, first published in 1968 and reprinted in 1974 and 1991. Sid, known as S G, died in 1974, aged 77.

Sid's son Anthony studied music at Keble College, Oxford. He became Reader in Composition at Hull University in 1962 until his retirement in 1995. In 1972 he was elected chairman of the Composers' Guild of Great Britain and was join-chairman of in 1973. A compact disc (CD) of his light orchestral music was issued in 1997 by Naxos/Marco Polo.

Anthony's daughter Fiona became a music teacher in Oxford.

While one part of the block was a cafe and once a motorcycle shop, the other main occupier was The Covent Garden Fruit Stores run by Arthur Butler, who can be seen outside on the left.

A portrait of Arthur Butler shows him outside the shop and his wife Edith show her lace making with a lace maker's pillow on a stand with the thread and bobbins.

Mrs Ann Painter recalls that her grandfather Arthur Butler had a shoe shop and a fish shop in Buckingham before he came to Bicester. The family lived at their Bicester shop where the ground floor included not only the shop area but a kitchen, dining room and sitting room. On the first floor were four bedrooms and then there was an attic above.

"There were also cellars where we did the washing and there was a bath. I believe the photographs of my grandparents date from the early 1930s. My father Caleb and his sister Annie, now Mrs Hunt, helped out in the shop. When my grandfather was taken ill during the Second World War Caleb and Annie ran the shop and continued until it was demolished," said Mrs Painter.

Bicester Ordnance Depot

The Ordnance Depot is outside Bicester parish but has had an impact on the town ever since it was built.

The Depot has been a source of employment and the need to house civilian employees created the first major housing estate in the town after the 1939-45 war.

It was built in 1941-42 to meet the urgent need of a nation at war. It became the largest military depot in the United Kingdom and was operational in time to support the Allied landings at Normandy and to re-supply the armies as they advanced through Europe.

The story of the Depot begins on January 31, 1941 when Col G W Palmer was instructed to find a suitable location for an ordnance depot that would play a vital role in the eventual return to Europe — D Day, June 6, 1944, as it turned out to be.

Col Palmer, who is commemorated by the road Palmer Avenue at the Depot, was told it needed to be in south-east England in an area bounded by Towcester, Warwick, Cheltenham, Swindon, Oxford and Aylesbury.

The Depot would need good road and rail routes, be near an RAF aerodrome and be in an area that offered some protection from the air.

With this remit, Col Palmer began his search. By May, 1941, he had selected farmland south of Bicester at Arncott and Ambrosden.

An advantage was that Arncott Hill and Graven Hill, Ambrosden, would help to disguise the Depot from the air. There is a story that has not been completely corroborated that the mists of Otmoor would assist the disguise.

In those days Bicester was well served by roads and by two rail lines: the GWR from London to Bicester and Banbury and LMS from Oxford to Bicester and Bletchley.

Another reason for the choice was that the agricultural land was low grade and would not affect the government's Dig for Victory campaign.

By June, 1941, the Treasury approved the spending of £5 million on what is the Base Ordnance Depot coupled with Bicester Garrison.

First on the site were the Royal Engineers and the Royal Pioneers, whose construction teams had to prepare the perimeter, drain and clear ditches and begin building the 42-mile internal railway.

On August 12, 1942, the first stores were issued from the Depot.

When the Depot was built Bicester had a population of 4,500 — compared with a military population of 24,000, supporting the Depot and garrison.

In the early days the Depot was not without teething problems. The water provided by the then Buckingham water authority dried up and water had to be imported in bowsers — small tanks — from the Upper Heyford airfield until another borehole could be sunk.

Electricity too was in short supply and many warehouses could only be used in daylight hours.

As Bicester was a small town trains were run to Oxford, London and Birmingham for leisure or leave trips.

The announcer at the London Marylebone station would say that a train was leaving for Bicester and give the names of the eight stations within the Depot.

Col Palmer was the first commdant of the Depot and commander of the Garrison. He became a Major General in 1945.

While the Depot handled hundreds of demands for supplies, not everything could be handled by the Depot in the early years.

Between 1943 and 1945 civilians in neighbouring villages were enlisted in what was called a Home Industries scheme.

In June, 1943, the use of voluntary civilian labour was being developed as a partial solution to a manpower problem at the Depot.

School authorities in Bicester released 18 schoolchildren, aged from 12 to 16 years, to work for three hours on Saturday mornings to assist in the making and packing of cartons. Their level of output was some 7,000 items in each of the three-hour shifts.

The scheme was expanded with Home Industry Centres set-up within local communities. Village halls and church rooms became the centres and by February, 1944, it was recorded that more than 1 million separate items had been packed by the centres. In May, 1944, it was reported by BBC radio one o'clock news that for that month 7.5 million articles were cartoned and 450,000 cartons packed and sealed. In December, 1944, over 100 million items had been cartoned since the scheme began. More than 900 people in villages and towns had contributed to this effort.

To support the scheme a daily "milkround" of stores, cartons and packaging materials were delivered to the local centres. Finished packed articles were collected in exchange for new items delivered.

The scheme ended in August, 1945. The Garrison newspaper, The Bicastrian, reported in November, 1945, on the winding up party of the Brill centre. The 130 strong centre had handled 16,600,000 items and packed them into 1,600,000 cartons.

After the war and general demobilisation a nationwide recruiting drive was launched to bring civilian staff to replace the military.

As part of this drive the War Office was responsible for building in conjunction with Bicester Urban District Council 850 houses at King's End and Glory Farm areas of Bicester.

In addition 550 houses were built in Ambrosden for military personnel and their families. Some additional housing was also built at Arncott.

While civilian staff were drawn from all parts of Britain, some 1,800 European Voluntary Workers (EVWs) were employed. The EVWs were people mainly from Poland and eastern Europe who were displaced by the war. They were allowed to live in England and at first were housed in a Nissen hut camp on Graven Hill. In recent years many were housed at a specially built group of bungalows at Greenfields, Arncott. Others married and integrated into the local community.

Since the 1939-45 war the Depot has increased in importance as it began to take in stores from other ordnance depots that closed down, for example Chilwell Depot outside Nottingham.

The Depot now supplies many stores to all three of the services, Army, Royal Navy and RAF.

The Queen made official visits to the Depot in 1965 and 1978. In 1977 as part of the Queen's Silver Jubilee Bicester Town Council granted Civic Honours to the Central Ordnance Depot, Bicester, which was roughly equivalent to granting the freedom of the town.

In 1992 units serving the Depot were amalgamated into the Royal Logistic Corps. These were the Royal Army Ordnance Coorps, the Royal Pioneer Corps, the Royal Corps of Transport and the Army Catering Corps.

Statistics are part of the life of the Depot. When it was built 29 miles of sewers were constructed, 27 miles of water mains, 40 miles of internal railway track, 20 million bricks were used, 20,000 tons of steel, 100 miles of electric wiring, 32 miles of surface drains, 75 acres of roads and hard standings were built.

The Depot covers 12 square miles and there are 38 major warehouses.

In 1992 the Bicester Advertiser reported that the Depot housed £259 million worth of supplies. There were 70,000 different types of times or item headings.

Of the supplies carried 60 per cent were classified as general supplies, 20 per cent clothing and 20 per cent motor transport items such as vehicle spares.

In 1992 there were about 1,600 civilians and about 900 military personnel.

The Depot supplies a wide range of stores from clothing, tentage to nuts and bolts. It does not supply ammunition nor military vehicles, which are handld by other depots, including Donnington Depot in Shropshire.

1942: A view from Ploughley Road, which runs between Ambrosden and Arncott, looking towards the engineer camp. The railway line linking Graven Hill at Ambrosden to Arncott is in the centre right bottom going towards the centre right.

The view above C site. The railway system is in place but site clearance has only been carried out for the storehouse locations with some Depot roads under construction. In the top left Palmer Avenue can be seen with site clearance work. The engineer camp at below centre left has become the site of the Depot headquarters.

The view above Arncott Woods. The rail network has been built and can be seen through C site and onwards towards Graven Hill. Site work for the construction of C site storage buildings is in progress. The hill slopes around Arncott Wood contain nissen hutted camps. The wood is still intact but later more woodland was cleared as the site for St George's Barracks, Arncott, in the middle distance.

1942: Camp accommodation was with 600 Nissen huts for soldiers. This is an interior of a typical hut showing the single stove providing basic heating.

ATS girls were often given the job of repairing to good as new condition air respirators and anti-gas capes. Pte Joan Halfpenny, from Swansea, is re-assembling the facepiece and fitting the outlet valve to a respirator.

When the Allies were preparing to launch their invasion they needed vast quantities of equipment. This photograph shows the build-up of ammunition at the Depot, which no longer supplies munitions.

Brass and metal buckles, buttons and other accessories are being cut off unserviceable articles by these women to be salvaged for re-use later.

Men relax in the sunshine at the Depot.

Lorries in open air storage.

The Garrison Theatre, Graven Hill, was one of several built at the ordnance depot for the entertainment of the troops. It was used for as a cinema and for stage shows. In recent years it has also been the scene of Army boxing tournaments, club dog shows, remembrance Day ceremonies and for amateur theatricals.

Track maintenance and repair on the internal railway.

Brill village Home Industries winding up party in 1945.

Present day storage and collection of items. Compare with the handling of ammunition in earlier photograph.

The hazardous stores warehouse, also showing present day warehousing.

The Queen and the Duke of Edinburgh at St George's Barracks, Arncott, in 1965.

The Queen at a garden party during her 1978 visit.

Part of No 2 camp that became the site of HM Prison Bullingdon in 1991-92.

An aerial view of Bullingdon Prison, 1992. Since it was built another wing has been added to the prison.

SECTION FIVE

Bicester Grammar School

Bicester County Grammar School opened in September, 1924, in Bicester Hall, the large property on the corner of London Road and Launton Road that is now Hometree House flats for senior citizens.

The school continued there until 1963 when it was transferred to new buildings adjoining Highfield Secondary School on a site off Queen's Avenue. The grammar school ceased its separate existence two years later when the two schools became Bicester Comprehensive School, known mostly as Bicester School and subsequently Bicester Community College from September, 1987.

Before becoming the Grammar School the house Bicester Hall had a fairly long history.

The house is believed to have been built in the first half of the 19th century and it is known from a Bicester directory to have been in the possession of Baron William Henry John Shroeder from 1874. His wife laid the foundation stone of the old St Edburg's Hall, on the corner of London Road and Priory Road, in 1882.

Bicester Hall became the hunting box of the Earl of Cottenham towards the end of the last century. The Earl was a Master of Bicester Hunt.

Mrs Margot Coker, of Bicester House, was reported in the Bicester Advertiser of February 8, 1978, as saying that the Earl originally took the house as a furnished property. He is believed to have extended the property with the addition of a stable block, dated 1896, behind that is now The Courtyard Centre, Launton Road.

In 1901 the new owner of the mansion was Mr Roland Hermon Hodge, of Rousham.

Mr Hodge was the owner when the property was taken over as a convalescent hospital in November, 1914. The first commandant at the hospital run by the Red Cross was Miss Esther Hendrick, daughter of the local Dr Hendrick.

Miss D Mountain (see Sheep Street) was among the Red Cross workers there and she recalled in 1978 that the first patients arrived soon after the hospital opened. It had beds for 50 patients, including soldiers recovering from gas poisoning, shell wounds and local soldiers and airmen, including Canadians and Americans who were building the Upper Heyford and Bicester airfields.

The YMCA built a wooden hunt in the grounds, which the troops used for recreation. It was also used for concerts and dinners given by local traders and others for old folk.

The hospital remained until 1919 when Bicester Hall was bought by Oxfordshire County Council from the then Col Hermon Nodge.

A report by the county education committee in January, 1924, said the stable block was originally intended for use as a Central School and the house as a Secondary School. The stables were then being used as a cookery, woodworking and school gardening centre.

Two months later it was announced that Bicester County - later Grammar - School would open in September, 1924, and fees would be ten to 12 guineas a year. There would be ten free scholarships.

When the school opened there were 43 pupils, 28 boys and 15 girls. The first head was Mr John Howson.

Mr Ewart Clothier joined in 1925 and became head in 1941. He told the Bicester Advertiser in 1978 that the long porch at the front was demolished for road widening soon after the end of the 1939-45 war.

Mr Clothier retired in 1963 and had been chairman of Bicester Urban District Council in 1956, 1960, 1961 and 1966. He died in 1991.

Mr Clothier was succeeded by Mr Stanley (Bill) Percival, who was in effect head of both the Highfield Secondary Modern School and Bicester Grammar School, which by then had moved to its new site. Mr Percival amalgamated the two into Bicester School. After he left Bicester he became head of a teacher-training college at Ambleside, Cumbria and was awarded an OBE in 1983.

As well as occupying Bicester Hall the Grammar School also had an annexe in Claremont House, a couple of doors away. The ground floor of Claremont House was the library with classrooms on the first and second floors. The top floor was a flat for three women teachers.

Mr Harry Hovard, a teacher, who became a deputy head and acting head at the community college, recalled that when the pupils had a fire drill they had to walk out on to the roof of Claremont House and on to the neighbouring building of Dean's, ironmongers.

"The women teachers in the flat also had a type of sling with a seat that was their fire escape. But we did not make them use it for fire drills," he said.

School, Bicester.

Bicester Hall. After the Grammar School moved out it became the offices for the Departments of Employment and Social Security. In the late 1980s the house was sold and in 1986 McCarthy and Stone began converting it into flats for senior citizens, renaming the property Hometree House. Flats were also built on the grounds at the back. But part of the grounds were also built on to create Bicester Day Care Centre, which was officially opened in May, 1988. A pilot day care centre was run in rooms at the stable block, The Courtyard. The stable block also housed youth activities and rooms also housed Bicester Citizen's Advice Burueau until they moved to The Garth in 1998. For a time the gardens were used for a young people's adventure playground with the Flying Fox aerial runway. But this ceased when the day care centre was built. The runway transferred for a time into Garth Park. A plaque on a nearby building reading Bicester Hall is erroneous.

Bicester Red Cross Hospital at Bicester Hall, showing nurses and patients. The photograph is dated 30-5-1915.

War wounded at Bicester Hall.

Red Cross nurses.

Red Cross nurses, Miss Dorothy Mountain is first left, on the front row. The men in the second row are believed to be, from the left Mr J T Mountain, Dr Hendricks, Dr Long and Dr Montgomery.

The first photograph of pupils and staff of Bicester Grammar School.

A rooftop view of the Grammar School and the hut.

The tunnel through the stable block showing the grounds and wooden hut beyond.

The grounds under snow, winter 1946/47.

The wooden hut in later years.

A classroom at the Grammar School.

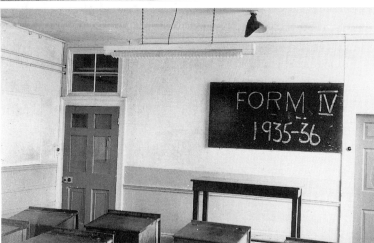

An unusual momento of Form IV, 1935-36. Many of the pupils went on to contribute to the public life of the town. For example, Vic Redfern became treasurer of Ploughley Rural District Council and an organiser of Bicester Sports Club galas/carnivals. Tudor Jones became a World War 2 bomber pilot and afterwards became a teacher at Bicester School and was chairman of the trustees of Bicester Sports Association.

A boxing ring set up inside the stable block, now known as The Courtyard Centre, dated 1941-42.

Girl pupils enter the ring to give a gym display. 1941-42.

Theatricals were part of school life with the formation of The Bicester Grammar School Staff and Old Scholars Dramatic Club, which ran from 1929 to 1963, with performances in the wooden hut. The photo shows the cast of *HMS Pinafore,* which was staged with The Cheerful Knave, in 1932.

In 1960 J B Priestley's celebrated comedy *When We are Married* was stage. From the left: John Schofield, Jimmy Schofield, Cliff Nash, Arthur Hollis, Brenda Wood, Tudor Jones, Freda Clothier, Brian Clifton, Margery Hyslop, Ruth Williams, unknown, Vic Redern, Judith Honeybone.

The cast of *The Farmer's Wife* in 1935: from the left: E T Clothier, D M Greenaway, L E Windsor, M Thompson (seated), T Jeacock, D J Worgan, T Satterly, J N Davies, G Harris (seated), D Vanstone, E M Fryer, E M Clothier, J L Howson.

Arsenic and Old Lace was performed in 1959. From the left: Tudor Jones, ? Brinkley, Jimmy Schofield (halfway up stairs), Arthur Hollis, Cliff Nash, Jimmy Davies (seated), ? Hyslop, M Hyslop (seated), Ewart Clothier (seated), Brenda Wood, Brian Clifton (policeman), Ron Hodges (policeman), Richard Owen (seated in front), Vic Redfern, Betty Alderson.

Sport naturally was a major part of school life. This photo shows the rugby team of 1946. From the left, back row: Roy ?, Chris Thomkind (2), Cecil Rhodes, Paul Jeacock, ?, David Stockley, Les Lambourne; front row: ?, Laurence Nash, John Hudson, Tom Hudson, Cliff Nash, Ken Lewis, Peter Winter, Brian Brain, Dennis Grace.

The 1947-48 rugby team. From the left, back row: E T Clothier (head teacher), Roy Dagley, Tony Hedges, Paul Jeacock, ? Miller, Chris Tomkins, Tony Merry, Les Jones (sports master); centre row: Gerald Taylor, David Stockley, Lawrence Nash, Peter Butler, Peter D Adams; front row: Harry May, ? Roberts, Geoff Shaw, Ian Hurle, Chris Bonfield.

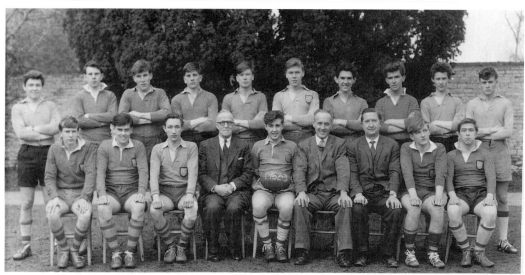

The rugby team of 1962-63. From the left, back row: unknown, Stephen Hughes, Stan Savins, Richard Wood, Michael Waine, Lawrence Brown, Bill Dodd, Ian Blackman, Royston Shentall; front row: John Malins, Henry Evans, Sean Hughes, Ewart Clothier (head), Malcolm Sawyer (capt), Leslie Jones (games master), Harry Howard (maths teacher and assistant games master), Andrew Banks. Malcolm Sawyer became a professor of economics at Leeds University. His parents kept a grocer's shop at the northern end of Sheep Street. Henry Evans took over the Evans Store, Andrew Banks became an architect and designed Hanover Gardens old people's flats in Manorsfield Road.

The 1st XV rugby team of 1963-64 was one of the school's most successful. The team played 15 matches, won 12, lost two and one was drawn, points for 134, points against 54.

From the left: back row: D W Corbridge, D H (Henry) Evans, K Mason, G S B Dew, R J Jones, P R Allen, S G Savins, M J Hudson, Steve Hughes; middle row: Sean Hughes, L R Jones, W E J Malins (capt), S W Percival (head), Andrew Banks (vice-capt), Harry Hovard, W E Dodd; seated on the ground: S N Taylor, D S A Yule, G F J P Murphy, S J Simmonds.

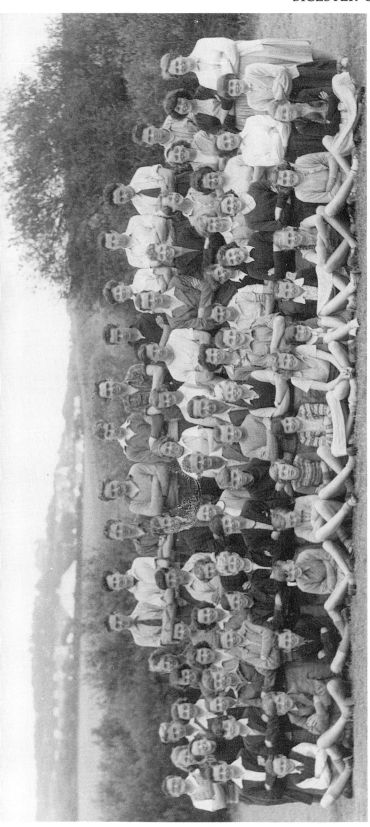

In the 1950s groups of pupils went on week-long summer camps to Whitecliffe Bay, Isle of Wight. The camp site was used by other schools. From the left, back row: Peter Price, Robert Clifton, R Moss, Tom Richens, Ron Barnard, Brian May, John Haynes, Patrick Aves, Brian Harding, unknown, Max Pemberton, David Penn, Christopher George; next row: Betty Griffiths, Mary Tomlin, Margararet Wood, Jeanette Waine, Brian Tomlin, Hugh Clifton, Pauline Eames, Gillian Allmond, Paul Berry, Kenneth Clarke, Huw Davies, Joan Roberts, Barbara Gardiner, Paul Crook, Wendy Head, Joan McCaulay; next row: Sarah Eales, Valerie Freeman, Sylvia Barnes, unknown, Pamela Raynsford, Mrs B Wood, Mr Frank Wood, Mr Harry Hovard, Mrs Eira Waine, Olive Cotter, Jean Gibbons, Gwenda Raynsford, Angela Hook; next row: Francis Blake, Tony Mant, Philip Scott, John Patterson, David Pearce, Robin Hughes, Geoffrey Tomlin, unknown, Derek Holmes, Brian Gebbells, David Steele, Ann Scotney, Linda Hann, unknown, Muriel Parker; next row: Stuart Forrest, Pete Goss, Colin West, Richard Wood, unknown, Pamela Butt, Enid Waine, Jackie Patterson, Judith Waine, Philippa Mouncey, Gillian Freeman, Julia Nicholson, Margaret Sansome.

Another camp at the same period. From the left: back row: Patrick Aves, Robert Clifton, Robert Harris, Paul Crook, Peter Price, Christopher George, Terence Burtonwood, Pauline Eames, unknown, Sylvia Barnes; next row: Margaret Wood, Gillian Mond, Michael Hermon, Mrs B Wood, Mr Frank Wood, Mrs Eira Waine, Mr Harry Hovard, Jeanette Waine, Eileen O'Connell; next row: Max Pemberton, unknown, Frank Blake, Michael Hedderley, Brian Tomlin, Jean Gibbons, Patricia Lovell, unknown, Barbara Gardener; front row: Enid Waine, Derek Homer, David Pearce, Robin Hughes, Judith Waine, Richard Wood, unknown, Brian Gebbels, John Patterson.

Ewart Clothier.

John Howson, first head.

SECTION SIX

Farming

Agriculture has been a prime industry for Bicester and district for centuries with ancient markets and fairs dating back to the 13th century. Most have lapsed over the years.

The town was once a centre for horse racing in the 18th and 19th centuries and has long been a home for fox hunting with the Bicester and Warden Hill Hunt, which became in 1985 the Bicester Hunt with Whaddon Chase when two hunts amalgamated. The opening in 1991 of the M40 motorway reduced the size of the Bicester country.

The Victoria County History of Oxfordshire records that local farmers sent butter, milk and other produce in huge quantities to London.

Livestock markets were held in the streets, King's End and Sheep Street, for many years until Bicester Urban District Council built a cattle market in Victoria Road, opening in 1910.

The cattle market at is opening, 1910.

The Nicholson family have farmed Manor Farm, Bucknell, since 1919. Archibald Frederick Nicholson, wearing a boater, is seen in his Straker Squire car at Farnham Royal, near Slough. The family had a brewery in Maidehead. The car was originally owned by Sir Roy Fedden, an aero engineer for Bristol Aviation. With Archibald is a son John Nicholson (seated next to him) and another son, Michael. The photo is dated 1913.

John Nicholson went to school at Winchester House, Brackley, and is seen with his father Archibald with a horse and carriage before leaving on the journey to school.

A threshing scene at Manor Farm before the 1914-18 war. The threshing engine was supplied by Mansfield and Rolfe, with Norman Rolfe in front of the engine.

The Nicholson children with the family Bullnose Morris Cowley car, 1924. John is seen with a dog, Michael is seated in the front with sisters Katherine and Mary in the back. Laurence is squatting in front of the rear wheel with Gerald. Laurence was a captain in the Oxon and Bucks Light Infantry and was killed in a glider airborne raid over the Rhine in the 1939-45 war.

Farming life was not all toil on the land. This photo dated 1927-28 shows the Nicholson family with friends in fancy dress for a party. Mrs Lillian Nicholson is seated in the centre, wearing a mortar board.

Wretchwick Farm, Ambrosden, dated 1915, was just outside the town on the London (Aylesbury) Road. It was farmed for decades by the Hadland family until 1971 when it was bought by Pavel (Paul) and Emma Friman. William Hadland had four daughters. In later years William Bunce helped to run the farm. He had a cottage on the other side of London Road. Mr and Mrs Firirman bought the farmhouse, barns and eight acres and later bought anoother five acres. They kept calves and Mrs Firirman bred and sold horses.

Happy haymakers at Wretchwick, July 28, 1917.

Farm workers at Wretchwick, 1889.

A family group in the garden at Wretchwick, August 1917.

Men of the family and presumably friends set off from Wretchwick on a shooting party, undated.

Two members of the farmhouse, 1911.

Feb. 1918.

An interior of the farmhouse, 1911.

The Allen family of Hethe and Fringford were agricultural contractors. The founder of the business was Thomas Hanks Allen and the company was T H Allen and Sons. Thomas Hanks Allen lived at Croughton and later Fringford Mill, where the family were millers from 1909. Later the family moved to Hethe and Mrs Allen's son Thomas Henry Allen joined the business. Some of the sons worked for the Earl of Effingham at Tusmore Park. Thomas Henry Allen also lived at Newton Purcell. His son Gordon lives at Cottisford. The company and staff are pictured threshing at a local farm.

Building ricks at a farm.

Members of the family and company.

Sheep dipping at a farm.

Road mending was another job undertaken by the family. All the Allen photographs are reproduced from glass plates.

A Changing Tapestry

Housing growth has brought the biggest changes in the tapestry of Bicester's life.

Some estates like Southwold, Langford Village the King's End Farm/Greenwood Homes are easily dentifiable. Less so are some of the smaller developments.

One is the Barry Avenue area, sometimes known as The Star estate, presumably named after The Star pub on Bucknell Road.

Slade quarry off Bucknell Road c 1927. It was operated by Aubrey Watson, who had quarries elsewhere. Barry Avenue would be running across the foreground of this photograph with Bucknell Road on the other side of the cottage.

Another view of the quarry operation.

George Titchener, pictured with his wife Maud on their golden wedding in 1912, was one of the main developers of the Barry Avenue estate that was built on the quarry site.

He came to Bicester in 1935 from Reading to work with developers Scrivener, who built Buckingham Crescent houses off Buckingham Road. After service in the 1939-45 war he was

foreman to Bicester builder Bill Rhodes, working on extensions to Corpus Christi College, Oxford. Following a spell in East Anglia he returned to Bicester in 1952 setting up his own company. He built houses in Blackthorn Road and West End, Launton, and Brashfield Road, Bicester. When he developed the quarry area off Bucknell Road he named roads after family and friends. Graham Road and Barry Avenue are named after his sons, Maud Close after his wife, Margaret Close after Mrs Margaret Wright, Raymond Road after Raymond Bainton, clerk to Bicester UDC and town council and also a town and district councillor and town mayor. Titchener Close is after himself. George was associated with Bicester Town Football Club for 40 years and was president for many years. One year the club did exceptionally well and he paid for players and their wives to take a day trip to Cheddar Gorge and Weston-super-Mare. He died in 1994.

Bicester Hunt has long been part of the town scene with traditional Boxing Day meets in Market Square. This photograph shows the hunt in Sheep Street passing the Crown Hotel on the left, probably in the 1920s or earlier.

Bicester Hounds are also holding a meet outside Old Place Yard House, Old Place Yard with St Edburg's parish church on the left.

The old open air swimming pool off The Causeway, was built in 1933 partly to give unemployed in the Depression jobs. A local committee was formed with Albert Lambourne as chairman. It remained in use until Bicester and Ploughley Sports Centre was opened in 1970. The area became a demolition site in the 1970s, followed by the building of Manorsfield Road and the block of shops and offices, including the National Westminster Bank.

The Vicarage & Church Terrace, Bicester.

The Vicarage and Church Terrace is seen probably in the 1920s. Recent research dates the now Old Vicarage as among the oldest houses in the town, describing it as a "hall house" whereby the main room was like an ancient hall, open for at least two storeys.

Priory Road, Bicester.

French & Son
Stationers
Bicester

Priory Road, Bicester, showing the junction with Chapel Street, once Water Lane. Priory Lane (behind the house at the bottom) was once part of the old turnpike into Bicester from London.

Bicester North railway station, Buckingham Road, was opened in 1910 when the Great Western Railway in conjunction with Great Central Railway, built the line between Princes Risborough and Aynho junction to give GWR a shorter route between London and Birmingham. GWR trains before had to use the longer route through Didcot and Oxford.

Bicester Town, formerly Bicester London Road, station was on the LMS Oxford-Bletchley service that was opened in 1850.

The building of the line north of Bicester to Aynho. This photograph is captioned on the back: Steam navvy at work digging out the cutting on the new line of the GWR near Bucknell, April 1907.

The Regal cinema in London Road was the town's only purpose built cinema. Until then the town's cinema was in a back room at the Crown Hotel. Sheep Street, and films first came to Bicester in a portable sideshow cinema with Thurston's fun fair in the Market Square in August.

The Regal opened in 1934 but by the 1970s the week was divided between films and bingo. It later became a full-time bingo club and finally closed in 1987 when the site was sold to a development company in Kidlington. The Regal was demolished in 1988 to make way for a block of flats.

Tom Martin was a projectionist at the Regal when this photo was taken on the cinema roof in about 1938. Tom is standing over the manager's office. When he was at the cinema the daily rushes for the science fiction film Things to Come were screened at the Regal as it was the nearest to the location filming at RAF Weston-on-the-Green.

REGAL CINEMA
LONDON ROAD
BICESTER
TELEPHONE: BICESTER 169

DIRECTORS:
JOHN MAXWELL (CHAIRMAN)
W. D. SCRIMGEOUR
E. LIGHTFOOT

UNION CINEMAS LIMITED.
Registered Office:
UNION HOUSE,
15, REGENT STREET,
LONDON,
S.W.1.

26th. August 1939.

TO WHOM IT MAY CONCERN.

The bearer, Thomas Martin, has been 3rd. Operator
at this Theatre for 2 years. During that time he
has proved himself to be a trustworthy, willing and
capable worker. He was able to carry through all
work appertaining to the Operating Box at this Theatre.

Signed _J.J. Smith_

Manager.

Tom left the Regal in August, 1939, to work in his first London cinema the Ideal in Peckham. He then went to the Globe at Plumstead but returned to Bicester in 1940 because of the London Blitz.

Tom worked at the Crown and earned this letter of commendation from the hotel proprietor A Tilt. Tom later returned to London and was a projectionist at the Granada, Tooting. He was often called to Granada's offices in Golden Square, Soho, to project rushes for Sidney Bernstein's film production company. Among the directors he met was Alfred Hitchcock. The Crown cinema was burned down during a fire in the 1939-45 war.

TEL. 23.

R.A.C. & A.A.
APPOINTED.

CROWN HOTEL,
BICESTER.

Sept 25th 40.

Dear Martin,
Thanks for your letter with
furtherance to your employment at Bicester.
If you care to come up as soon as possible
I can start you as second operator & relief
at the terms mentioned £I-I-per week & full
board with us.
I can assure you that the job should be
more congenial than working for a Circuit.
and I think you would find it homely.
Please let me know when you can start & I
should like to know your exact age.
Yours Faithfully,
H. Tilt Prop,r.

Staff of Bicester Post Office are seen in Market Square in 1915. The PO was later moved to a new building in Sheep Street.

Sport was always a big part of town life. The Bicester Young Men's Club team is pictured in the 1945-46 season. From the left, back row: F Scarrott, M Wall, E Austin, J Vinall, K Smith, W Ware, J Collett, D Murray; front row: A Simons, F Timms, P Scott, V Houghton (capt) S Gregor, R Haynes, J Baughan.

The Bicester team that won the Chipping Norton hospital cup in 1925.

Bicester Detachment of the Oxford Voluntary Reserve on January 7, 1917.

Bicester Bowls Club is among the oldest sporting clubs in the town. The team here, back left F Gordon, G Harris, front left T Green, A Baker won this cup in an Oxfordshire tournament in 1915. Players with the club won the trophy next in 1998.

Parish Church and Methodist Church

St Edburg's church, pictured in 1885, dates from the 12th century and stands outside the site of the earlier Bicester Priory, which covered the area known today as Old Place Yard.

In A Short History of Bicester Priory (1983) David Watts says the priory was founded in 1182 by Gilbert Bassett in his park behind the Causeway. In 1536 the priory was dissolved and the priory church demolished. Cloister buildings that remained were demolished in 1673.

Mr Watts also records that in 1978 David Farmer suggested that St Edburg of Bicester was probably the daughter of King Penda of Mercia. This Anglo Saxon princess worked as a nun at Adderbury and Aylesbury and was believed to haved died c AD 650. It may be assumed that the bones of St Edburg - spelt variously as Edburga or Eadburgh, were obtained for the shrine from her original place of burial at Bicester or nearby. The shrine was in the priory church but was removed to Stanton Harcourt parish church during the demolition of the priory church in 1536 by Sir Simon Harcourt.

St Edburg's parish church is among the oldest buildings in the town, along with the neighbouring Old Vicarage and the Old Priory in Priory Lane, which could be all that remains of a hospice.

Leaping forward over the centuries brings us to 1963 when this photograph was taken outside St Edburg's Church after a Sunday morning service.

The photograph was taken to mark the launch of a second Christian Stewardship campaign covering 1964-67 when money was raised to complete St Edburg's parish centre of two halls in Old Place Yard. The halls were opened in 1967 but were demolished in 1992 to make way for a block of flats. The barn that formed part of the larger of the two halls has been converted into a smaller parish hall.

A key identifies many people in the phtograph:

1 Margaret Hudson

4 Thomas Hudson,
   churchwarden and magistrate

6 Philip Hudson

7 Cyril Kinch, *bellringer and
   outfitter in The Causeway*

8 Wilfred Hunt, *verger*

12 Ted Evans, *bellringer*

17 Mrs Ray Kendall

20 Mrs Driscoll

21 Margaret Driscoll

22 Rose Bown

23 Mrs Trebble

26 Mrs Evelyn Harris,
   jeweller, Sheep Street

27 Elizabeth Smith

29 Vera Allen

30 Master Blossom

31 John Hollis, *deputy Lord
   Lieutenant and variously town
   district and country councillor*

35 Michael Waine, *now head of
   Glory Farm primary school
   Bicester*

36 Rev Cannon W Henry Trebble,
   vicar of Bicester

38 Arthur Hollis, *teacher*

41 Mrs Hunt, *verger's wife*

42 Nellie Hayes, *school and Sunday
   School teacher*

44 Mrs Philpot, *widow of Bert
   Philpot, undertaker, who
   emigrated to Vancouver when she
   was 80 to join son John and lived
   to be 100*

47 Eva Spence

53 Ray Kendall

54 Major Arthur Fane MC, *after
   whom Fane House, St John's Street
   was named*

55 Joan Waine

56 Pamela Driscoll

57 Mr Martin.

A procession from the church to St Edburg's primary school to mark the first renovation of the school in the early 1960s. Michael Waine leads with the cross and the Rev John Goddard, vicar of Launton, is on the left in front.

In September, 1967, an ordination for deacons was conducted by the Bishop of Dorchester, the Rt Rev D G Loveday, Among the new deacons was Michael Charles Scott-Joynt (standing on the right at the back with quiff of hair over his forehead). In 1975 Mr Scott-Joynt became vicar of Bicester in succession to Canon W H Trebble, who retired in 1974. During his time Bicester Mr Scott-Joynt became Rural Dean of the Bicester and Islip Deanery. In 1981 he left to become a canon of St Albans cathedral and became the youngest bishop in the Church of England when he was appointed Suffragan Bishop of Stafford in 1987, aged 44. As Suffragan Bishop he was an area bishop in the Lichfield diocese. He became Bishop of Winchester in 1995, gaining a seat in the House of Lords. Canon Trebble is on the left of the Bishop of Dorchester in the photo with the Rev John Goddard on the right, below Mr Scott-Joynt.

Although the Methodist Church in Sheep Street was opened in 1927, Methodism in the town dates back to 1814 when Mrs J Bowerman and her husband opened a room in a farmhouse in Sheep Street for worship. The building was later adapted into Wesley Hall. A Wesleyan Church was built in 1840.

The Wesley Hall in Sheep Street was eventually sold to Woolworth's in 1955 and is now a furniture shop. Woolworth's later moved to their present location. The Wesleyan Church in North Street was sold in 1925 to become Weyland Hall, home of a Masonic Lodge.

Much of the site of the present Methodist Church was bought in 1919. The church is officially the Grainger Hargreaves Memorial Church, named after the Rev Grainger Hargreaves, who was minister from 1921-23. He was a missionary in China.

When the church was planned it was going to have a tower, but this was never built.

One aspect of the Methodist Church that many remember was the Red Rythmics Harmonica Band, formed in 1936 as a musical activity for the Sunday School. The first performances was for a Sunday School concert and the first London appearance was at Whitcfield's Tabernacle Methodist Sunday School workers' gathering.

Sid Hedges, Sunday School leader, was conductor. About 18 months after its formation the band made its first BBC radio broadcast from Birmingham and also broadcast in London from Central Hall, Westminster, and Kingsway Hall. The band did not play during the 1939-45 war and was revived in 1948. It was eventually disbanded in 1957. Members wore red berets, ties and belts and white shirts or blouses and grey trousers or skirts.

Over the years the line-up changed but included George Rose and Joe Leach, who became a prominent councillor.

This picture dates from the later years. Sid Hedges is on the left with Wilf Smith on drums. In the back row from the left is Sid's son Anthony (accordionist), Maurice Alley, Ron Hughes, Bette Baughan, Jeanette Redfern, Ivan Hoare, Mary Orchard, Joyce Murray (double bass); front row, from the left: Norman Coward, Percy Allsworth, Derek West, Les Blackman, Mary Coward.